Kate Loves to Skate

by Liza Charlesworth • illustrated by Anne Kennedy

SCHOLASTIC INC.

New York • Toronto • London • Auckland • Sydney
Mexico City • New Delhi • Hong Kong • Buenos Aires

Designed by Grafica, Inc.
ISBN: 978-0-545-68616-7
Copyright © 2009 by Lefty's Editorial Services.
All rights reserved. Published by Scholastic Inc.
SCHOLASTIC, LET'S LEARN READERS™, and associated logos are trademarks
and/or registered trademarks of Scholastic Inc.

12 11 10 9 8 7 6 5 4 3 2 1   14 15 16 17 18 19/0

Printed in China.

The Ate Family

What Is a Word Family?
A word family is a group of words that rhyme and share the same spelling pattern, such as *Kate*, *skate*, and *gate*. Read this story to learn more *–ate* words!

Meet **Kate**.
Kate is a member of the **Ate** family.

Kate loves to **skate**.
There she goes through the **gate**!

Kate loves to **skate**

with a penguin named **Nate**.

Kate loves to **skate**
with a penguin named **Nate**

and a **crate** of **date**s.

Kate loves to **skate**
with a penguin named **Nate**
and a **crate** of **date**s

and spaghetti on a **plate**.

Kate loves to **skate**
with a penguin named **Nate**
and a **crate** of **date**s
and spaghetti on a **plate**

when the hour is **late**.

What does **Kate hate**?
Falling down!

Poor **Kate**.
What a **state**!

Word Family House

Point to the *-ate* word in each room and read it aloud.

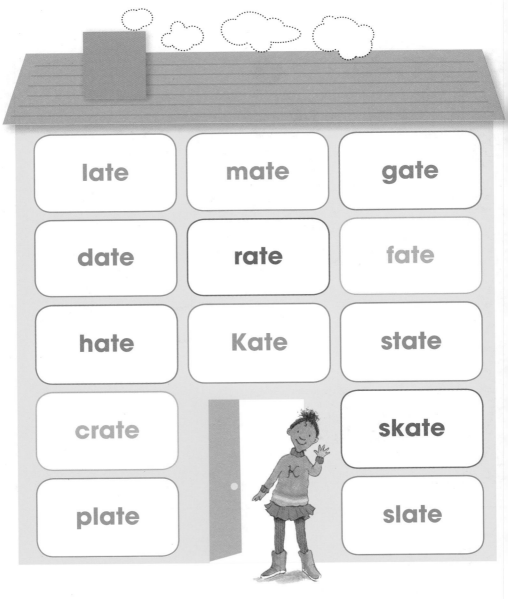

late	mate	gate
date	rate	fate
hate	Kate	state
crate		skate
plate		slate

Word Family Match

Read each definition. Then go to the plate and put your finger on the right *-ate* word.

Definitions

1 part of a fence

2 to dislike

3 to glide across ice

4 a wooden box

5 the opposite of *early*

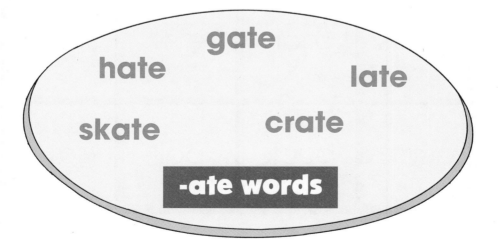

gate
hate
late
skate
crate
-ate words

Word Family Bingo

Which words belong to the *-ate* family? Cover them with buttons or pennies. Get four in a row to win!

fate	pick	well	date
bell	rate	prank	plate
sank	snail	spell	state
crate	buck	pail	gate